Advanced Praise for

PEARLS OF GOLD

"One of the most profound and critical thinkers of the 20th and 21st centuries, Verna Linzey has written a masterpiece, *Pearls of Gold*, which is a must-read."

—*Manuel A. Biadog, D.Min.*
Poetic & Wisdom Literature Reviewer, NTV Bible

"Verna Hall Linzey portrays . . . a path toward light in a world that can host plenty of darkness and reminds the reader how welcoming spirituality can be."

—*Kirkus Reviews*

"Be refreshed, prepared, and challenged by what is written here."

—*Alveda C. King, Ph.D.*
Recipient, 2021 Presidential Lifetime Achievement Award

"Verna Hall Linzey's collection of poems will bring a smile to your soul. More than that, they will aid you in contemplating the wonders and perplexities of God and His creation."

—*N. Blake Hearson, Ph.D.*
Book Review Editor, Midwestern Journal of Theology

"Here you will find wisdom and encouragement."

—*Raul Mock,*
Executive Editor, The Pneuma Review

"These poetic treasures will inspire moments of quiet reflection for Verna Linzey's readers."

—*Mark H. Ellis,*
Senior Editor, Assist News Service

PEARLS
of GOLD

The Poetry of Verna Hall Linzey

FOREWORD BY ALVEDA KING

JAMES LINZEY PUBLISHERS

Tulsa, Oklahoma

James Linzey Publishers
7122 S. Sheridan Road
Tulsa, Oklahoma 74133
www.LinzeyPublishers.com
(760) 855-3905

ISBN: 978-1-936857-51-7 (Hardcover)
ISBN: 978-1-936857-52-4 (Trade Paperback)
ISBN: 978-1-936857-50-0 (eBook)

Library of Congress Control Number: 2023922675
Manufactured in the U.S.A.

Cover and Book Design by Glen Edelstein, Hudson Valley Book Design

To my son,

Jim

CONTENTS

FOREWORD

WHEN PERIPHERALS COLLIDE, convergence is imminent.

The life of Verna May Hall Linzey is a gift from God, and I am honored to pay tribute to her by way of this foreword. Her long and fruitful life will continue as a memory in our hearts as we read her book.

Verna was a prolific writer, songwriter, Bible translator, movie actress, television and radio host, crusade evangelist, speaker, singer, and recording artist. She spoke for conventions, conferences, crusades, and seminars in Haiti, India. Japan, Mexico, the Philippines, Singapore, the United States, and the United Kingdom. This remarkable woman devoted her many gifts and talents to God, with lasting results.

Verna once said: "The way people live creates their past, present, and future. The trajectory of one's journey through life is unique to each individual, and creates a distinct story."

As a "Creative Christian," Verna was blessed to share truth in prayer, poetry, and a myriad of expressions. Her "pearls of gold" were forged in the fire of the Holy Spirit, and reflect the affections, perceptions, and conceptions that came alive with her unique breath of creativity.

If we dare to follow the paths she blazed, we may see ourselves reflected in some of her poetry, and become emboldened to forge paths of our own.

In this book, Sister Verna not only shares her poetry, but she also generously shares her life, as reflected in her words. I salute Sister Verna for her insightful and delightful works. Her poem, *Kindness*, strikes a chord for me as a theme for this season in my life.

I encourage you to dive in. Select your favorites as you drink from the fountain. Be refreshed, prepared, and challenged by what is written here. May God bless your next steps on your journey.

—*Alveda C. King*

Dr. Alveda C. King is the daughter of the late slain civil rights activist Rev. A. D. King and the niece of Dr. Martin Luther King, Jr., as well as a Christian evangelist. Additionally, she is the founder of Speak for Life. She is also an acclaimed author, television host, and film and music veteran. Dr. King is a former Georgia State legislator, Chairman of the Center for the American Dream for AFPI, and a 2021 recipient of the Presidential Lifetime Achievement Award. Please visit her at: www.alvedaking.com.

PREFACE

THE WAY PEOPLE LIVE CREATES their past, present, and future. The trajectory of one's journey through life is unique to each individual, and creates a distinct story. Consequently, we all have unique experiences to share that can enrich the hearts of others who may be watching our stories unfold. Some tell their story through the eyes of a third person; some tell it through their own eyes. Others tell their stories allegorically, and some biographically.

My desire is to share my life poetically, prayerfully, and perceptively, and the way I have chosen to live is reflected in these "pearls of gold." Some of these pearls reflect on how I perceive people and God, as well as my faith in them. Other pearls reflect on how I experience life with a hope of inspiring my reading audience with a zest for life and the expectation that their story can be what they want it to be. Still, other pearls mirror whom I have chosen to become.

I trust that you may see in some of these pearls of gold a reflection of the way you would like the story of your life to become, a hope for a better future in the way that only you can dream, and that you will be empowered to step forth and write the history that you would like to live.

—*Verna May Hall Linzey*

ACKNOWLEDGMENTS

MANY PEOPLE WHO HAVE READ my poetry and expressed their favorites have had an impact on the final selections for this book. They are truly appreciated.

In particular, I would be remiss not to mention Jimmie Rodgers and Pat Boone for their friendship and inspiration when exchanging lines now and then with them backstage and when performing together. I deeply appreciate my friends Kathy Lee Gifford and Debbie Boone for their encouragement, thoughts, and reflections. And finally, I would like to thank Janet McKeighan for her camaraderie and cheering me on in life.

There are many others, too numerous to enumerate, whose joyful countenances have always showed me the best face of humanity, which have served to remind me that there is intrinsic value to each experience with people about which is worth writing.

—*Verna May Hall Linzey*

CHRISTMAS

Guardian Angel by Lindberg, 1901
Alteration by James F. Linzey, Copyright © James F. Linzey 2019

Angels

Angels are sweet
   With comfort divine,
And very discreet;
   I know one is mine.

The Church Yard by Edmund Koken, 1862

No known restrictions on publication.

One Wintry Night

'Twas a wintry night
And quite dark and cold,
In the dead of night,
   In an open wold.

A poor, homeless child
   Saw a lighted abode.
Quite meek and so mild,
   He greatly extolled,

"I'll knock on the door,"
   With heart filled with joy.
A man opened it wide,
   And said, "Welcome home, boy!"

His eyes fill with tears,
   This poor little lad,
For to his surprise
   He found his grand Dad!

The Annunciation to the Shepherds by Govert Flinck, 1639
No known restrictions on publication.

The Holy Night

On the holy night
  In heaven so far,
The shepherds did see
  A very bright star.

The power of God,
  This story of old,
Was all about Christ,
  Of whom angels foretold.

The Adoration of the Magi by Peter Paul Rubens, 1634
No known restrictions on publication.

The Three Magi

Three wealthy magi came from afar
To pay their respects to the newborn King.
It took them two years to follow the star;
Treasures of gold and spice did they bring.

When from the Mideast they then did arrive,
The star from the East finally stood still.
Now at the house, where the Child did abide,
Prophecies of old did the magi fulfill.

They bowed to the ground, their faces to touch,
Presenting Him gold, to support the Christ Child;
They then gave Him myrrh and frankincense much,
To support Him while He lived in exile.

The three wealthy magi departed for home,
Leaving the Child—to Egypt He roamed.
Avoiding King Herod, who died on the throne,
The Christ became King, as angels foretold.

EASTER

The Ascension by Rembrandt, 1636
No known restrictions on publication.

The Ascension

He rose from the grave,
    Death he defied;
After forty more days,
    He ascended on high.

He told them to stay
    In Jerusalem 'til
The Spirit, He prayed,
    Our world He would fill.

He gave up the shroud,
    And tossed it away,
And went in the clouds
    To heaven to stay.

The Crucifixion by Carl Heinrich Bloch, 1870
No known restrictions on publication.

The Crucifixion

Nailed to a cross with such impunity,
Suffering scourge and so much wickedness,
And reflecting the sin of a vile humanity,
Christ bore our sins with all willingness.

He paid the price for the fall of mankind;
There's much more to do when He soon returns.
This was the plan to restore Paradise,
The season of which you may discern.

The Last Supper by Leonardo da Vinci, 1495-1498
No known restrictions on publication.

The Last Supper

He sat at the table quite solemnly,
To have one last meal before He would die;
With just his best friends, and no family,
He did some strange things that were ritualized.

A big meal was served; of course, there was bread.
He took it and said it was Him crucified.
He talked about blood of the New Testament;
They then had their wine, the fruit of the vine,

Then Judas, the spy, left in a big rush,
When the rest had all asked, "Lord, is it I?"
Minding the order, "Just get it all done!"
He put on his cloak and then said, "Good bye!"

One saddening supper, costing His life,
Drops of His blood came forth from His brow.
Up from the grave He finally did rise;
So, all of my sins I now disavow!

The Resurrection by Rembrandt, 1638
No known restrictions on publication.

The Resurrection

The Resurrection—
    Most powerful feat,
Three days in Hades
    Chose He to go;
To death and to life
    Obtained He the keys;
So now unto Him,
    Oh, how we do owe!

The Transfiguration by Peter Paul Rubens, 1604-1605
No known restrictions on publication.

The Transfiguration

As Jesus was praying
    On top of the mountain,
Two radiant beings
    Stood and did blazon.

Disciples were watching—
    Dumbfounded were they—
While God began saying,
    "Hear what He does say!"

GENERAL

A Church in Winter by Louis Apol, 1900
No known restrictions on publication.

Age

The older you get,
 The more you'll become
Aware that the rest
 Are very lonesome.

But trusting in Christ,
 The older you get,
The more you'll be wise,
 And more just like Him!

A Saint from the 'Jackdaw of Rheims' by Briton Rivière, 1868
No known restrictions on publication.

Blackbird

Blackbird hears the voice of God,
    Singing to her a sweet new song—
"Come to the fountain and drink from me,
    Rest in my presence and sing to me!"

Blackbird obeys the voice of God,
    Flying to hear this brand new song;
She lands on top of the Word of God,
    Feeling the power of the presence of God.

She sees the cross of Him who died,
    The Lamb of God who bled and died;
Blackbird learns this song of God,
    Giving praise to Him, the Creator of all.

"In Your presence is fullness of joy,
    At Your fountain is water for all!"
Composing this hymn that she enjoys,
    Blackbird sings her song to God.

Blackbird hears the echo of God,
    Who repeats to her His sweet new song—
"Come to the fountain and drink from me,
    Rest in my presence and sing to me!"

"My fountain of rest is filled with joy,
    My presence, so rich, for you to enjoy!"
Having sung to her His sweet new song,
    Blackbird obeyed the voice of her God.

The Country Stream by Louis Aston Knight, 1903
No known restrictions on publication.

Charity

Although I speak
    Like men and like angels,
With charity sweet,
    Ringing like bells,
Such oracles deep
    Come forth from my mouth,
In tenderness meek,
    And never too loud.

Christ Our Pilot by Warner Stallman, 1950
Christ our Pilot © 1950, 1978 Warner Press, Inc.,
Anderson, Indiana. Used with permission.

Courage

Facing the fear of death,
    Facing the loss of friends,
Facing evil events,
    What courage in the end!

The Prodigal Son by Eugene Bernand, 1888
No known restrictions on publication.

Don't Ever Give Up

When you face trouble
　　Which others have caused,
Cling to the gospel
　　And pray for their flaws.

Expressing God's love,
　　And never complaining,
Don't ever give up!
　　Be ever constraining!

The Town Square by Edmund Koken, 1864
No known restrictions on publication.

Eternity

Eternity seems
   Like life filled with cheer;
Perhaps it may be
   Forever despair!

You may not be sure
   Which way it will go;
So just go to church,
   And then you will know!

Puget Sound on the Pacific Coast by Albert Bierstadt, 1870
No known restrictions on publication.

Excellence

The Beauty of Creation—
    How Excellent!
The Wonders of the Oceans—
    How Eminent!
The Majesty of Mountains—
    How Envisaged!
The Miracle of Salvation—
    How Evident!

A Country Stroll by Carl Bletchen, 1835
No known restrictions on publication.

Faith

Faith sees a way
    In the darkest night,
Showing the light
    Where the sun won't shine;
It cuts a path
    For the lame and blind,
And says a prayer
    For the darkened mind!

The Philosopher at Home by Rembrandt, 1632
No known restrictions on publication.

Faithfulness

The faithfulness of a friend,
  Like a cool wind
    On a warm summer night,
Is really true-heartedness.
  It heals the soul
    And enlightens the mind!

Daniel in the Lion's Den by Briton Riviere, 1892
No known restrictions on publication.

Forbearance

Forbearance from action,
Showing stoicism
And lenient toleration,
Resists criticism.

The Child on a Forest Path by Camille Pissarro, 1859
No known restrictions on publication.

Gentleness

The gentle touch
Of a springtime breeze
Flowed through the leaves
Of the forest trees,

Across the path
Of a child who saw
It touch the face
Of a loving God.

Ocean Sunset by Ivan Aivazovsky, 1841
No known restrictions on publication.

God

God Omniscient—
  How knowledgeable of us!
God Omnipotent—
  How powerful for us!
God Omnipresent—
  How available to us!

Shipwreck at Sea by Hovhannes Aivazovsky, 1850
No known restrictions on publication.

God Is

God is transcendent—
    How unreachable from us!
God is immanent—
    How reachable to us!
God is immanently transcendent—
    How pervasive for us!

The Praying Girl by George Frederick Watts, 1887
No known restrictions on publication.

Goodness

Virtue and rightness,
   Morally speaking,
Are all about goodness,
   And rejecting bad things!

A Winter Home by August Eduard Schleicher, 1877
No known restrictions on publication.

Home Sweet Home

Winter for rats,
    Springtime for birds;
Summer for cats,
    And Autumn for worms!

Whichever you are,
    Wherever you go,
You'll never be far
    From Home Sweet Home!

Christ at Heart's Door by Warner Sallman, 1942
Christ at Hearts Door © 1942, 1970 Warner Press, Inc., Anderson, Indiana.
Used with permission.

Humility

In the fear of the Lord
  One finds humility;
Then simple, little doors
  Open eternally!

The City Gate by Louis Apol, 1888
No known restrictions on publication.

I Will Pass One Time

Through this life
　　I will pass one time;
I will sacrifice
　　Each day.
To Him I will yield
　　To have new life,
For life is death,
　　But death is gain!

Jesus Walking on the Water by Ivan Konstantinovich Aivazovsky, 1888
No known restrictions on publication.

Integrity

As beauty is to a flower,
    So, integrity is to a man;
It draws virtuous people to him,
    And allows him to righteously stand.

The Adoration of the Shepherds by Guido Reni, 1640
No known restrictions on publication.

Joy

The thrill of the moment
   Is a fleeting moment's pleasure;
But the joy of the Lord is
   A longer, lasting treasure!

Head of Christ by Warner Sallman, 1941
Head of Christ © 1941, 1968 Warner Press, Inc., Anderson, Indiana.
Used with permission.

Love

The love of God
    Mends a broken heart,
Arriving on
    The wings of a dove.
Soothing your soul
    Wherever you are,
His power, so rich,
    Has come with such love!

The Woman in Prayer by Rembrandt, 1635
No known restrictions on publication.

Meekness

Meekness is patience,
   Gentleness too;
Longsuffering, Mildness,
   And charity true.

Docility, diffidence,
   Modesty real;
Humility, lowly—
   'Tis very ideal.

Christ in the Manger by Fillipo Lippi, 1459
No known restrictions on publication.

O Blessed Jesus

O Blessed Jesus, our precious Savior!
He came from Heaven to die for me.
He was resurrected and went to glory;
He promised to come again for me.

He prayed the Father to send the Spirit,
The promised Holy Ghost, to comfort us.
Our Lord empowers us to tell to others
Of Jesus' love and saving power.

It may be evening, it may be morning,
He'll guide us to that new-made shore;
He'll take us with Him to dwell forever.
Oh, what a gathering, to part no more!

He prayed the Father to send the Spirit,
The promised Holy Ghost, to comfort us.
Our Lord empowers us to tell to others
Of Jesus' love and saving power.

A Maiden at Work by Louis Aston Knight, 1892
No known restrictions on publication.

Patience

Calmly working in the breeze,
   Gently sweeping up the leaves,
And slowly pulling all the weeds,
   Buys you honey from the bees!

Verna May Hall Linzey, 1941

Pearls of Gold

Pearls of gold
    Come forth from her lips,
For she is quite old,
    Endowed with great wit.

A blessing is she,
    This pearl of gold,
For she does foresee
    The pitfalls of old.

The youth who are wise
    Will enter her fold
And pray at her side
    With pearls of gold.

This mother of pearls,
    To those who aren't old,
Will teach them in turn
    With lips of pure gold.

The youth who return
    Will spiritually grow,
For she helps them learn
    With pearls of gold.

The Temptation of Christ by Ary Scheffer, 1854

No known restrictions on publication.

Power

Power is not
  Who you say you will be!
Power is not
  What you hope you will be!
Power is
  Who you are indeed!

Sanctae Trinitatis by Bartolome Esteban Murillo, 1682
No known restrictions on publication.

Sanctae Trinitatis

The Father—
    The head of three Persons divine!
The Son—
    The incarnation of the Father divine!
The Spirit—
    The presence of Sanctae Trinitatis divine!

The Old Man by Rembrandt, 1652
No known restrictions on publication.

Self-Control

Restraining yourself
   While tempers unroll
Will anger dispel
   In your self-control!

The Praying Man by Eric Enstrom, 1918
No known restrictions on publication.

Temperance

Moderation in action,
Restraining your passion,
And cessation of friction
Show discretion and temperance.

Lighting the Candles by Peter Paul Rubens, 1617
No known restrictions on publication.

The Beautiful Soul

The beautiful soul
　　With charity sweet,
Sparkles like gold
　　In children so meek.

The Deluge by Francis Danby, 1840
No known restrictions on publication.

The Flood

With no regard
for God's righteousness,
The Lord gave them warning
To turn from their sins.

Not heeding the call
God gave unto them,
The rain that came down
Had been sent from Him.

But Noah found grace
In the sight of the Lord,
The judgment of whom
Came not upon him.

An ark did he build
With so much reward;
All of the sinners
God finally did rid.

The Lighthouse by Vilhelm Melbye, 1872
Alteration by James F. Linzey, Copyright © James F. Linzey 2019

The Lighthouse

The fog rolled in on the sea one day,
As the shipmates prepared for the voyage.
The crew could not see as they sailed away,
But soon passed under the drawbridge.

Out on the sea the waves grew high;
The ship, she was strong and was ready.
The tempest grew stronger as time went by,
But slowly she sailed and was steady.

Then down came the rain, and how it did thunder!
No more was she safe out at sea.
In a night and a day would she make it to harbor,
If soon a fast clip made she.

But then did she falter; oh, did she whine,
While lost in the night out at sea!
And behold, a lighthouse was seen in the night;
She finally made it to safety.

A Winter Day by Gustav Hausmann, 1877
No known restrictions on publication.

The Wildwood Church

There's a small wildwood church in the country so far,
With windows alit by the Spirit of God.
And the people inside—they know no despair,
For they trust in the Lord and rest in His care.

Church bells ring each Sunday, the Day of the Lord,
And when they do pray, they sing all the more;
Revival is there, you can truly be sure.
So, bring all your cares, to the small wildwood church.

Then one Sunday morning in the small wildwood church,
The people grew quiet, as they read in the Word:
For God so loved the world that He gave His dear Son.
It is Him they do serve, while living in love.

Church bells ring each Sunday, the Day of the Lord,
And when they do pray, they sing all the more;
Revival is there, you can truly be sure.
So, bring all your cares, to the small wildwood church.

A Man and a Girl by Josephus Laurentius Dyckmans, 1861
No known restrictions on publication.

Things

Nice things we say,
   Nice deeds we do,
Will day by day
   Make us like You!

Christ in Gethsemane by Heinrich Hofmann, 1886
No known restrictions on publication.

Thy Will

To do Thy will, O Lord, is good;
    A favor one will find.
Amidst the love of brotherhood,
    A man will find new life.

The Light of the World
by William Holman Hunt, Manchester Version, 1856
No known restrictions on publication.

Trust

Trust in the Lord
   With all your might;
He'll open the door,
   And show you the light.

HUMOR

The Fight by Joos van Craesbeeck, 1646
No known restrictions on publication.

Kindness

Kindness for me
   Is showing some love;
Forgiveness sweet—
   That kind of stuff!

Don't pull your hair,
   Or scrap or fight;
But do say your prayers,
   And just say, "Good night!"

The Dog and the Saint by Briton Riviere, 1869
No known restrictions on publication.

The Saint

One day the saint walked down the street,
    To breathe the air that God did make;
He then got knocked right off his feet
    By Spot, the dog, who licked his face!

But then the dog walked down the street,
    To breathe the air that God did make,
When he got knocked right off his feet,
    And quickly clobbered by the saint!

The Cat and the Rat by Adolf Von Becker, 1864
No known restrictions on publication.

The Storm

During the night
   There rose a great storm.
She turned on the light
   And screamed like a horn!
For under the bed
   She saw a big rat,
Lie dead in its sins,
   Caught by the big cat!

PATRIOTIC

The Washington Monument, courtesy of the Department of Defense

A City of Faith

O Lord, our veterans fought for the land of the free,
A beacon of hope, promise and light,
A City of Faith from sea to shining sea,
In a world filled with tyranny and the darkest night.

For the valor of our veterans,
We consider their memorable lives,
Preserving freedom for Americans
While placing in jeopardy their own lives.

Remind us, O Lord, the meaning of freedom.
Equip us with strength to follow their ways,
Should we be called to sign up and be one,
Who fights for God and country all of our days.

Iwo Jima Memorial, courtesy of the US Marine Corps

Pax Americana

The American Armed Forces
    Preserve God-given peace;
It continually forges
    Divine liberty.

May God in love divine,
    For America's preservation,
Continually refine
    Pax Americana.

PRAYERS

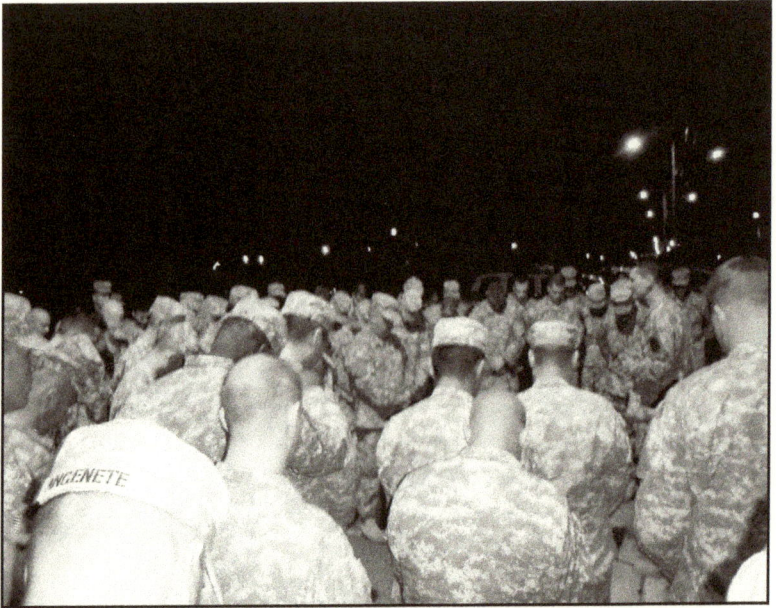
Deploying Soldiers, from Fort Dix, New Jersey, to Iraq
Courtesy of Chaplain, Maj. James F. Linzey, USA, September. 3, 2007

A Prayer for Deployment

Almighty God, prepare the hearts and minds of Thy servants as they deploy. In the midst of danger, we humbly beseech Thee that Thou wouldst grant them safe passage to their destination, though they travel through danger. Grant them peace and refuge in Thy tender care. Guide them always into Thy gracious word to find wisdom and knowledge, serenity, and truth. Be with their families, strengthening them in separation. And reunite them once again, we pray, in Thy tender love. Lead the command to seek Thy ways, bringing liberty and peace, and justice for all. In Thy name we pray. Amen.

Queen Elizabeth II on her Coronation Day
By Cecil Beaton, June 2, 1953
Royal Collection RCIN 2153177

A Prayer for Her Majesty Queen Elizabeth II

On Becoming the Longest Reigning Monarch in British History
The 9th of September 2015

Almighty and most gracious Father, for our security, Thou hast given long life to Her Majesty Elizabeth II, and placed her as the longest reigning monarch in British history. Grant peace and prosperity to the United Kingdom, and her Realms, Territories, and Commonwealth. We petition Thee to keep Her Majesty, your humble daughter, in the palms of Thy gentle hands all the days of her life. Illuminate her mind, continually granting her wisdom to lead Thy people well; through Jesus Christ our Lord. Amen.

Her Majesty Elizabeth II, Goddard Space Flight Center, Maryland
By Eric Draper, courtesy of NASA, May 7, 2007

A Prayer for Her Royal Majesty Queen Elizabeth II

On the 90th Year of Her Majesty's Birthday
The 21st of April 2016

Almighty and most merciful Father, for our heritage, Thou hast entrusted into the stewardship of Her Majesty Elizabeth II, the United Kingdom, and her realms, territories, and Commonwealth. We humbly beseech Thee that Thou mightest grant her Thy blessings of prosperity and the power to keep us free from oppression, with secure borders, shores, and skies. Deliver the United Kingdom, and her realms, territories, and Commonwealth from discord, disloyalty, envy, pride, and every sort of evil. Grant that Thy people and her subjects and servants would rise to the aid of Her Majesty to fight for freedom, hearkening to her voice, ensuring unity under Thy will. Grant her peace and wisdom, and lead her subjects and servants into obedience to Her Majesty's will that we may be a light to the world, a light on a hill which cannot be hid, that she may glorify Thee before the nations of the world. And when she is tried, let not Her Majesty's faith fail Thee. Let not Her Majesty grow weary in well doing, but let her grow stronger with each passing trial; through Jesus Christ our Lord. Amen.

United States Marine Corps Color Guard
By Cpl Chi Nguyen, USMC, courtesy of USMC

A Prayer for the
United States Armed Forces
November 11, 1947

Almighty God and most merciful Father, we ask You to impart by Your Spirit to the men and women serving in the United States Armed Forces, as well as to our veterans, an illumination of their spirits and minds, revealing to them the need for the Savior Jesus Christ. Convict of sin, O Lord, those who stray from righteousness, chastising them as only a loving Father would do, until they receive the atonement that is only wrought by the blood of Jesus Christ, who alone provides for the propitiation of their sins, and repentance brings them to the foot of the cross, and Your Spirit reigns in and through their mortal flesh.

Let freedom of the one, true religion of faith in Christ alone, and salvation in no other name under heaven, be expressed freely and openly in the United States military, throughout the ranks, that all military men and women may hear the gospel, and draw nigh unto You, O Lord, and be saved. We ask for an eternal reward for those who have served. Bless our veterans, meeting all their needs—those and their loved ones who have sacrificed everything, so that we may enjoy freedom of religion throughout the land, from which all other freedoms emanate. In Your name we pray. Amen.

Changing of the Guard at the Tomb of the Unknown Soldier
Sgt. Benton Thames, Sgt. Jeff Binek, and Spc. William Johnson
Courtesy of Sgt. Erica Vineyard, USA, December 24, 2005

A Prayer for
United States Veterans

Almighty God, we thank You for our veterans who have risked their lives to preserve our great heritage—our nation and the rich freedoms we enjoy. Our veterans remind us that freedom is not free, that each generation must preserve her. Let us not take for granted that which other people never had. But let us be willing to honor our veterans' heroism by also placing our lives at risk for freedom's sake, if need be, lest their sacrifices be made in vain. Amen.